DAVID ANSON RUSSO

GO FOR IT!

RACES, RESCUES, TREASURE HUNTS AND MORE

A MAZEMASTER BOOK

SIMON & SCHUSTER BOOKS FOR YOUNG READERS
Published by Simon & Schuster
New York London Toronto Sydney Tokyo Singapore

SIMON & SCHUSTER BOOKS FOR YOUNG READERS
Simon & Schuster Building, Rockefeller Center
1230 Avenue of the Americas, New York, New York 10020.
Copyright © 1992 by Mazemaster David Anson Russo.
All rights reserved including the right of reproduction
in whole or in part in any form.
SIMON & SCHUSTER BOOKS FOR YOUNG READERS
is a trademark of Simon & Schuster.
Manufactured in Singapore

10 9 8 7 6 5 4 3 2 1

ISBN 0-671-73350-8

Welcome, adventurers!
The mazes in this book will take you on
exciting journeys filled with hidden perils. There is one
trail—with several connecting paths—to the
finish. The connecting paths are in very
unexpected places, so keep a watchful eye
—and good luck!

THE RULES

Follow the trails from start to finish. You may
travel under any trails or through any barriers that
have double arrows. Jumping from trail to trail is
prohibited.

LOST IN THE JUNGLE

The jungle hides many surprises and dangers. Make your way across streams filled with poisonous snakes and keep a watchful eye for the ferocious cheetah, the pack of hyenas, and the leopard about to pounce. If you make it, we'll see you at the outpost!

START

JUNGLE CAMP

TRIBAL RIVER

HUNTING JACKALS

HERD OF HAPPY ELEPHANTS

VULTURES

HYENAS

WILD BOAR

ZEBRAS

WATERING HOLE

HIPPOS

PYTHON ON ROAD

SPIDERS

CHARGING RHINO

TRADING POST

LOWLAND RIVER

VULTURES

BAT CAVE

KUDU LOOKING FOR A DRINK

LION FAMILY

DANGER BITING FISH

SPIDERS

CROCODILE

HOP THE STONES

JUNGLE OUTPOST

QUICKSAND

SUPPLY BOAT

FINISH

CIRCUS SURPRISE

You are driving a fire engine through a three-ring circus to save the clowns from a burning building. Go for it—but watch out for the alligator and the ferocious lion.

START

MAGIC

STILTS

RINGMASTER

ELEPHANTS

JUGGLERS

THE FAMOUS PERFORMING STALLIONS

TIGERS

THE DOG SHOW

ZEBRAS

THE
FEROCIOUS
LION AND
HIS
TRAINER

TRAPEZE

CIRCUS
ANIMALS

SNAKE
CHARMING

THE HIGHWIRE ACT

PLAYFUL
BEARS

SEALS

THE BURNING BUILDING

OOPS

FINISH

BIGFOOT RUN

Get out your backpack and trail mix—you must climb the highest peak of the mountain range. Watch out for bears, wolves, moose, bald eagles and Bigfoot. Use your compass and don't get lost.

START

EAGLES

DUCK POND

BIGFOOT

BIGFOOT

ROCK SLIDE

RESCUE HELICOPTER

TROUT POND

CAREFUL BEAR

WOLVES

CLIMB A RUGGED MOUNTAIN

TRAIL HIKING

MOOSE

SHIPWRECK ADVENTURE

The shipwrecked galleon has lain on the sea bottom for centuries. Find the galleon's gold, but beware the dangers of the deep.

START

POISON STINGRAYS

SAW FISH

HAMMERHEAD SHARK

VIPER FISH

GIANT CLAM

JELLYFISH

MEAN FISH

SEA CRAB

TREASURE TRAILS

The red X marks the spot where the pirate treasure is hidden. Only one path leads to the treasure—if you can avoid the perils of the lost island.

START

QUICKSAND

SPIDER NESTS

GIANT OCTOPUS

HERMIT'S HUT

JAGGED REEF

PIRATES LANDING

PIRATES COVE

STRAIT OF PERIL

GIANT SEA TURTLE

WATCH OUT SLIMY SEA MONSTER

SHIPWRECK

DANGER IN THE DESERT

The desert is blistering hot. There is almost no water, but a lot of unfriendly creatures. You are out of water and must get to the oasis. Good luck.

START

DESERT WOLVES

YOU'RE OUT OF WATER

LOOKING FOR FOSSILS

HORNED LIZARD

SKELETON

TORTOISE ON THE MOVE

WATCH THE LIZARD

DESPERATELY DIGGING IN THE SAND

VULTURES

JACKRABBIT

GILA MONSTER

RATTLER

NIGHT HUNTING FOX

SPIDERS

HALLOWEEN ESCAPE

Hurry—run home before the clock strikes midnight! Snakes, spiders, witches, and monsters will do all they can to stop you.

WOLF

WITCH'S HOUSE

NO TRESPASSING

THIS MEANS YOU

KEEP OUT

PUMPKIN PATCH

START

THE INVISIBLE MAN